ESSENTIAL DK

P9-BYM-826

CHOOSING THE RIGHT STOCKS

MARC ROBINSON

DORLING KINDERSLEY

London • New York • Sydney • Delhi • Paris • Munich • Johannesburg

A DORLING KINDERSLEY BOOK

Writing Stephanie Rubenstein
Design and Layout Hedayat Sandjari
Photography Anthony Nex
Project Editor Crystal A. Coble
Project Art Editor Mandy Earey
DTP Designer Jill Bunyan
Photo Research Mark Dennis, Sam Ruston
Indexing Rachel Rice
Editorial Director LaVonne Carlson
Design Director Tina Vaughan
Publisher Sean Moore

First American Edition, 2000
2468109753

Published in the United States by
Dorling Kindersley Publishing, Inc.
95 Madison Avenue,
New York, New York 10016

Packaged by Top Down Productions
Copyright © 2000
Dorling Kindersley Publishing, Inc.
Text copyright © 2000 Marc Robinson
See our complete catalog at
www.dk.com

Dorling Kindersley Publishing, Inc. offers special
discounts for bulk purchases for sales promotions or
premiums. Specific, large quantity needs can be met
with special editions, including personalized covers,
excerpts of existing guides, and corporate imprints. For
more information, contact Special Markets Dept.,
Dorling Kindersley Publishing, Inc., 95 Madison Ave.,
NY, NY 10016; Fax: (800) 600-9098

Library of Congress Cataloging-in-Publication Data
Robinson, Marc, 1955-
Choosing the right stocks / Marc Robinson.–1st American ed.
p. cm.
Includes index.
ISBN 0-7894-6318-0
1. Investments–United States–Handbooks, manuals, etc. 2.
Stocks–United States–Handbooks, manuals, etc. I. Title.
HG4921.R53 2000
332.63'2042–dc21   00-031492

Reproduced by Colourscan, Singapore
Printed by Wing King Tong, Hong Kong

CONTENTS

INTRODUCTION

Investing in stocks can be very lucrative and it can be very frustrating. Knowing as much about what you are investing in, will help make it a more satisfying and perhaps successful endeavor. Choosing the Right Stocks will guide you through understanding what a stock is, what happens with stocks, how the markets work, how to analyze stocks from a variety of perspectives, ways to buy and sell them, and many nuances that will make your investment experience easier. This book will help turn what can seem like an overwhelming research project, into a manageable and rewarding experience.

UNDERSTANDING STOCKS

What is a stock? What do you do with stock? How can you buy or sell them? Knowing the answers to these questions will help you decide if investing in stocks is the right decision for you.

WHAT IS A STOCK?

*Y*ou *can be a business owner in virtually any industry you can imagine. Millions of people from all walks of life own companies that make the products you use every day.*

WHAT IS A SHARE OF STOCK?

The most important thing to know about investing in stocks is that a share of stock is a unit of ownership in a company. When you buy shares of a company's stock, you become a part-owner in that company and are called a *shareholder*. All of the decisions you make when investing in stocks should be based on your perspective as an owner of a company, making business decisions.

OWN ANYTHING ▶
Look around you. Products come from all sorts of companies. You can own part of those companies by owning their stocks.

WHAT DOES A SHARE REPRESENT?

One share of stock usually represents a very small percentage of company ownership. How much you own of a company depends, therefore, on how many shares you own. If, for example, you own 100 shares of a company that issued one million shares, you would own one-hundredth of one percent of the company. Many companies have issued tens, or even hundreds of millions of shares.

WHY BUY STOCKS?

Most people buy stocks to make money in one or both of these ways:

Price appreciation. When the price of your stock rises, the value of your investment increases.

Dividends. A company may share some of its earnings with shareholders by distributing *dividends*.

WHO ARE SHAREHOLDERS?

There may be thousands, even millions, of shareholders (also called *stockholders*) of one company's stock. Some of a company's largest shareholders may be the founders of the company, institutional investors, such as pension plans and mutual funds, or very wealthy private investors. By far, the largest number of investors in the country, however, are individuals like you who buy stocks in their personal accounts and in retirement accounts such as 401(k)s and IRAs.

> **I** Anyone can be a part owner in any company simply by buying its stock.

A STOCK IS BORN: IPOS

I ssuing stock is one way a company can raise money to expand its business. This decision signals a new beginning in the life cycle of a company.

SELLING OWNERSHIP TO THE PUBLIC

If a company wants to raise large sums of money without incurring debt, it can choose to issue shares of stock and sell it to the public. This is called *going public* and is done through an *Initial Public Offering,* or *IPO.*

With an IPO, the company's management decides to receive a major cash infusion it doesn't have to repay, and in exchange, allows the general public—anyone who wants to invest— to share ownership in the company.

WHY COMPANIES GO PUBLIC

Going public signals a major step for the growth of a company. Management has made a decision to reach for another level of competitiveness, using the money it raises from selling shares of ownership. It may hire more people, buy more equipment, expand research and development, increase production, enter new markets, and even use the money to raise awareness for its products through marketing and advertising.

WHAT THEY GIVE UP

Most of all, a company gives up its total control and privacy. From the moment it begins the IPO process, it's required by law to fully disclose everything about how the business operates, who operates it, what it owns, what it owes, and virtually anything else that a prospective owner/ shareholder would want to know before deciding to invest. After the IPO, the company is legally required to regularly file and release all kinds of information and will be closely scrutinized by the press, stock analysts, regulators, and members of the general public.

2 Going public turns a company from a closed book to an open book.

THINGS TO KNOW

- When the SEC clears a security for distribution, it doesn't mean that the SEC approves of the stock. The SEC ensures that all necessary information has been filed, but doesn't attest to the accuracy of the information, or pass judgment on the investment merit of the stock being issued. Any representation that the SEC has approved of the stock issue is a violation of federal law.

- It's usually not easy to buy shares in an IPO. Typically, you need a good relationship with a broker who belongs to the syndicate issuing the stock and has access to shares. Otherwise, most of the investors in an IPO are those with either an influential amount of money to invest or those who have a strong relationship with their broker.

- Much of the money from an IPO goes to the company. A significant portion goes to those who worked to bring the company public; mostly the underwriters and the lawyers.

HOW AN IPO WORKS

The company hires an investment banking firm, called the *underwriter*, who helps the company file a registration statement and preliminary prospectus (also known as a *red herring*) with the Securities and Exchange Commission (SEC), the governing agency for all securities activities. These documents must detail financial and business information about the company.

The underwriter agrees to pay the company a certain price for its shares. It then has to resell those shares to the public. If the underwriter wants to reduce its risk, it can share the underwriting with several other investment banking companies and brokers (a *syndicate*). The underwriters' fee is the difference between the price they pay to the company and the price they sell to the public.

Next comes a twenty-day cooling-off period. During this time, the stock may be discussed with potential buyers, but the preliminary prospectus is the only information permitted to be released.

If the SEC approves the registration statement, a final prospectus is issued. This contains all the information from the preliminary prospectus plus any amendments, as well as the offering price of the stock, and the underwriting fees. Now the shares may be sold in the IPO.

The underwriter must now sell all the shares or it will be stuck with them. The stock will now be for sale on the open market (also called the *secondary market*) to anyone that wants to buy it.

THE LIFE OF A STOCK

After the stock is made available to the general public for the first time in the IPO, it then is available for anyone to buy or sell.

TRADING BEGINS

When some of the original investors decide to sell part or all of their ownership, they offer shares for sale. New buyers invest in the company because they believe in its ability to grow and generate profits that can raise the stock price. But that isn't always what happens. No one can truly predict what will happen to a company's fortunes, so the life of a stock is a life of anticipation and speculation.

THE PRICE CHANGES

Stock prices go up and down as a result of the trading between buyers and sellers. At any point, the price of a stock reflects the price at which sellers are willing to sell, and buyers are willing to buy. A stockholder may sell because of a need for cash, an interest in owning another company, a change of goals or strategy, or a belief that the stock price will fall. Investors typically buy shares to have a say in the way the company is run, to receive income from dividends, or out of a belief that the stock price is going to rise.

STOCK SPLITS

If a stock price becomes too expensive, a company may announce a stock split. After a split, more shares are available for trading at a lower price. For example, after a 2-for-1 stock split, a company with one million shares selling at $100 will have 2 million shares selling at $50. Current stockholders will receive two shares for each share they own so the value of their shares remains the same. But new investors will be able to buy stock at $50 instead of $100.

REVERSE SPLITS

If a company wants to raise the price of its stock—whether to make it appear more expensive, to create less supply and more demand, or to eliminate small shareholders—it can announce a reverse split. For example, if a $1 stock reverse splits 1-for-10, the new shares will be worth $10. Current shareholders must trade in 10 old shares and receive one new share.

THERE MAY BE DIVIDENDS

A dividend is a share of the company's earnings paid to stockholders. The company's board of directors determines the amount of the dividend. Shareholders may receive cash payments, or if a company offers a reinvestment program, they may turn dividends into additional shares of the company's stock through a Dividend Re-Investment Plan (DRIP). In the past, paying a dividend signified the stability of the company. This is not necessarily the case anymore. The amount can rise or fall depending on the company's earnings. If earnings are up, the company may increase its dividend, which may make its stock more attractive to new investors.

TENDER OFFER

This is a public invitation to shareholders of a company by investors who wish to buy the company (in other words, a bid to take control of the company). After a tender offer, those who've accepted the offer surrender (*tender*) their shares in exchange for cash.

PUBLIC OWNERSHIP MAY END

Although in theory, a stock may live on forever, some stocks have shorter lifespans than others. Here are a few reasons:

Buyback. Companies can repurchase their own stock to regain some control by reducing public ownership. If earnings stay the same, fewer shares will result in higher earnings per share, which might cause the stock price to rise. Some companies announce buybacks and don't actually do them. They may boost the stock price.

Taking private. A company's management may decide they want more flexibility and independence for decision making and they no longer want to share their profits. If so, they will need to raise enough money to buy back all the shares held in public hands.

Merger. Two companies may believe they will be stronger if they merge. One company may buy all the shares of the other (giving the other's shareholders cash for their stock), or the two may create a new stock and issue it to all shareholders.

Takeover. A company may believe it can be stronger if it buys all the shares of another company and absorbs the assets and customers. A takeover can be friendly (both companies like the idea) or hostile (the target company will try to resist the takeover).

FORMS OF OWNERSHIP

A share of stock is a share of ownership that's been packaged to sell to investors like you. Different packages are created for different legal and business purposes. Here are the most common.

COMMON STOCK

Common stock represents the basic—and most common—type of ownership in a company. When a company goes public it must issue shares of common stock first. Typically, a company will issue many more shares of common stock than it will issue of any other type of stock.

Owning common stock gives you the rights that go with participating as an owner of a company. Most of all, when the stock price rises or falls, you participate in that increase or decrease. Usually, you have the right to vote on corporate issues, and you will share in any profits distributed as dividends to common stockholders. If the company goes bankrupt, all the creditors must be paid before common shareholders receive any proceeds because, as in any business, all those who loaned money are repaid before the owners are paid.

PREFERRED STOCK

Some companies issue a variation called preferred stock. In a stock listing, it's the one with a "pfd" after the stock symbol. The main reason companies issue preferred stock is to raise money at a lower cost than borrowing the money. In addition, preferred stock usually doesn't include voting rights.

Preferred stock tends to attract investors who are looking for a relatively low-risk way to receive fixed, regular income payments. The dividends are usually higher than dividends paid to the company's common stockholders, and if the company goes bankrupt, preferred stockholders will be paid before common stockholders.

3 Stocks are considered liquid investments, meaning they can be sold and turned into cash easily.

DIFFERENT CLASSES OF STOCK

Companies can issue different classes of common and preferred stock, typically labelled A, B, C, etc. Each class represents a different aspect of ownership and is used to raise money for a different purpose. One class may fund the acquisition of another company. Another might be issued to raise money without offering voting rights.

FOREIGN STOCK

American Depository Receipts (ADRs) make it easier for Americans to invest in shares of foreign companies. An investor receives a receipt for a share of stock in a foreign company that trades on a foreign exchange. The reason ADRs make it easier to own foreign companies is that they allow investors to buy and sell ownership in these companies in the U.S. markets using U.S. dollars. Without the ADR, investors could only invest in a foreign company by trading in a foreign country's stock market and converting their dollars to that country's currency.

Investor benefits. By buying ADRs, investors avoid unfamiliar rules of overseas exchanges, the complexities of currency exchange rates, and the investing laws of the country in which the stock trades.

Company benefits. Companies typically issue ADRs to increase the market for their shares, raise capital, and expand global exposure for their products.

4 Be sure that you understand the rights and restrictions of any preferred stock you consider buying.

A STOCK OR A BOND?

Despite its name, preferred stock typically acts and trades more like a bond than a stock. It pays a fixed amount as a dividend, the way a bond pays regular interest. It also normally fluctuates less in price than its common stock counterpart, providing stability more characteristic of a bond than a stock. Finally, like a bond, preferred stock usually has a temporary life. There may be a redemption date and price, meaning investors will receive cash for their shares at a specified date in the future.

GROUPING STOCKS BY INVESTMENT QUALITIES

*P*rofessionals are constantly categorizing stocks in order to find ways to predict their price behavior—and therefore, make money. Often, categories overlap each other. These are some of the most common categories that focus on the qualities of the stocks themselves.

INCOME STOCKS

Some stocks pay high dividends. These are usually well-established companies with steady earnings that are in the mature phase of their life cycle. The dividends are usually higher than interest you might get from a savings or money market account.

Investors buy income stocks to receive regular, predictable income with the expectation of more stable prices, not strong price increases.

Previously, utility companies were traditionally considered income stocks. As deregulation continues, utilities may become growth stocks, just as AT&T did when the telephone industry was deregulated in the '80s.

BLUE-CHIP STOCKS

These are stocks of companies with strong reputations, who dominate their industries, pay consistent dividends, and are expected to grow at about the same rate as the economy. They have long-term, consistent track records of solid earnings and growth.

VALUE STOCKS

These are typically stocks of strong, well-established companies whose price is lower than comparable stocks in its industry, thereby creating a *value* opportunity. They have steady earnings streams and may pay dividends. Because of their financial stability, they may be able to weather economic downturns better than many of their competitors.

PINK SHEET STOCKS

Some stocks don't meet the minimum criteria for listing on an exchange or on NASDAQ. Instead, they're listed in the Pink Sheets. The name comes from the days when quotes for these stocks were printed on pink paper. Pink sheet stocks are typically low-priced, and thinly traded, meaning you may not be able to buy or sell them quickly. and trading them is usually expensive. Information may be difficult to obtain because few analysts and newspapers cover the stocks. The Internet may be the best source for information on them.

GROWTH STOCKS

These are typically stocks that don't pay much of a dividend, but instead reinvest earnings to grow the company. The term "growth" actually refers to the outlook for a company's business. Investors tend to think of it in terms of growing the money they invest. A company doesn't have to be young to be considered a growth stock. It could be any established company that is well positioned for growth in a booming area of the economy.

Investing in a growth stock usually means you have to accept the potential for more unpredictable price dips and rises, than an investment in income stocks.

> **5** A blue chip stock that pays high dividends may also be considered an income stock.

SPECULATIVE STOCKS

These are the stocks of companies that typically have inconsistent, or no earnings, but are expected to produce substantial earnings in the future. Investors in these stocks are speculating with their money that a company will be successful and that the success will  translate into higher stock prices. Typically, speculative stocks are from relatively young companies in the *emerging growth* phase of their life cycle. The stock of an established company emerging from bankruptcy, could also be considered a speculative stock. What makes them so speculative is the lack of history on which to base future predictions.

GROUPING STOCKS BY BUSINESS QUALITIES

Here is a sampling of commonly used groups based on qualities of the companies who issued the stocks.

BY THE ECONOMY

Our economy tends to move in cycles of growth and recession. One way to look at stocks is by the way particular companies perform in various parts of the cycle.

Cyclical stocks. These are companies whose earnings are strongly tied to the overall business cycle of the country. They tend to do well in certain economic climates and not so well in others. This means that the prices of the stocks tend to increase as the economy grows and tend to decrease as the economy shrinks. They're typically consumer-driven companies in industries such as housing, automobiles, airlines, and publishing. American Airlines, Dell Computer Corporation, and Ford are all examples of cyclical stocks. These companies make products that are purchased more in a better economy and less in a worse economy. These stocks are best invested in when you believe the economy is going to grow.

Non-cyclical stocks. Often called *counter-cyclical*, these are companies who have relatively steady income. They make products people use no matter what the economy is doing. Eating, brushing your teeth, and washing your hair, for example, are things you do no matter what the economy is doing. Because they're not tightly tied to the ups and downs of our economy and can perform well in most situations, non-cyclical stocks are generally considered less risky than cyclical stocks. Non-cyclical stocks can be speculative, growth, value, blue-chip, or income stocks. It depends on the products they make.

ELASTIC OR INELASTIC ▶
Many of the products you keep around the house (like those pictured here) are considered non-cyclical, or inelastic. The amount they're used doesn't expand or contract based on people's income. Electronics, on the other hand, are considered cyclical, elastic products where consumer demand is affected by the amount of discretionary income people feel they can spend.

BY THE INDUSTRY

Viewing a stock from the perspective of its industry can be a great indication of how the stock may perform. However, never judge a stock by its industry alone. For example, the drug industry is considered a very solid industry for investments. Within the drug sector, however, there are companies that are considered speculative, growth, value, blue-chip, and income stocks. Their products are usually non-cyclical, but they may earn a large portion of their revenues from cyclical products. They may also be large, mid, or small cap. You need to consider all of these factors in order to make a sound investment decision. The best way to invest by industry is to choose the industry you believe will perform well, and then look closer at specific companies within that industry. Then choose a stock that fits your risk level within that industry.

BY TOTAL STOCK VALUE

A popular way to group stocks is by their size in the market. *Market capitalization* or *market cap* measures the total value of all shares of a stock in the market. For example, if a company has ten million shares in the market and each share is priced at $10, it has a market capitalization of $100 million. Stocks are loosely divided into four main categories by capitalization. These definitions have risen significantly in recent years, reflecting generally higher stock prices. As of March, 2000:

- Micro cap: Under $400 million;
- Small cap: $400 million to $1.75 billion;
- Mid cap: $1.75-11.5 billion;
- Large cap: Over $11.5 billion.

Why does market cap matter? It usually gives an indication of the strength of the company within the market. Typically, trading is easier in larger capitalization stocks, because there are more shares and shareholders than with smaller cap stocks. Many investors also believe that larger cap stocks are safer investments, over the long-term. Capitalization by itself is not an indication of the volatility or potential of a stock. Market capitalization is very important to a company because the more the company is worth, the easier it is to borrow money for the things they need to stay competitive (new equipment, research and development, staffing, etc).

17

UNDERSTANDING THE MARKETS

Many newcomers to stocks think of the stock market as one place. In fact, the stock market is a general term encompassing a variety of different organizations.

WHAT ARE THE MARKETS?

A stock market is any place where people can buy and sell their share of ownership in publicly owned companies. A stock market is part of a larger entity called the capital market, which is the term used to describe any place a business can go to raise money.

THE CAPITAL MARKET

Capital markets, with the help of financial institutions, bring together the demand for and supply of investment money. People and companies need to borrow money for things such as cars, homes, and other companies. Financial institutions make loans to fulfill these needs. Some of those loans are then sold as investments to the public who want to invest in them, because they hope to make money on their money by doing so. They may make money in the form of interest, as with bonds, or if the investment is traded (bought and sold in the capital markets), they may make money if the value of their investment goes up.

THE STOCK EXCHANGES

These are the organizations that control the trading of stock. Companies issuing stock must fit the criteria set by an exchange and then become members of that exchange. Their

shares then trade according to the rules of that exchange. The exchange has the primary responsibility for seeing that trades are conducted in a fair and orderly manner that is fair to all participants large and small. The exchanges regulate the issuers of shares (the companies) that trade on their exchanges and the investment dealers who trade shares on the exchanges.

THE STOCK MARKET

The stock market is the part of the capital market where the public goes to buy and sell ownership of many of the world's corporations. There are two levels of stock markets.

Primary market. IPOs (see page 8) are sold in the primary market—where stocks are initially offered to the public.

Secondary market. Once stocks are sold in the primary market, they become available for trading in the secondary market. This is the stock market as most people picture it. The stock exchanges, such as the New York Stock Exchange and Nasdaq, are the marketplaces for trading stocks in the secondary market.

6 The main reason companies go to the capital markets is to raise money.

WHY THE STOCK MARKET EXISTS

The stock market exists to bring investors who want to sell together with those who want to buy stocks. It offers a place where companies can raise capital and where investors can invest and speculate.

GLOBAL TRADING

Many countries throughout the world have their own stock markets. These markets often affect our markets and stock prices. Many stocks of United States companies are traded on these markets, which may account for price changes that occur after our markets close one day and reopen the next day.

THE AUCTION MARKET

The places where stocks trade are called exchanges. The original form of a stock exchange is the auction market.

WHAT IT IS

An auction market is a physical marketplace where traders come together face-to-face to buy and sell stock. They conduct their trades through a matchmaker known as a *specialist*. The specialist works at a booth on the *floor* of an exchange:

WHO WORKS ON AN AUCTION MARKET?

These are the main people involved in an auction market.

Floor brokers. These are people who are cleared to trade on the exchange floor. They receive the trading orders you place with your broker and conduct the trade with the specialist for that stock. Some floor brokers are employees of one firm. Others are independent and contract their services to a number of brokerage firms.

Specialists. These are people who are assigned to trading posts to keep the flow of orders running smoothly, matching buyers and sellers at fair prices. They also provide pricing information.

Each exchange has strict trading guidelines. Specialists are subject to fines and censures if they fail to conduct trades properly. Each individual specialist handles approximately 8-9 stocks. The most heavily traded stocks have one specialist devoted solely to them.

NEW YORK STOCK EXCHANGE

The New York Stock Exchange (NYSE), located in New York City, is the largest auction marketplace in the world. As of March 2000, there were over 3,000 stocks listed on the NYSE.

Listing requirements. (As of September, 1999) A stock listed on the NYSE must generally have a minimum of 1.1 million shares publicly held by at least 2,000 round lot (increments of 100 shares) stockholders. The publicly held common shares should have a minimum combined value of $18 million. The company should have net income in the latest year of over $2.5 million before federal income tax and $2 million in each of the preceding two years.

AMERICAN STOCK EXCHANGE

The American Stock Exchange (AMEX), also located in New York City, lists over 700 companies and is the country's second largest auction marketplace.

Listing requirements. Regular listing requirements for the AMEX include pre-tax income of $750,000 in the latest fiscal year or two of most recent three years, and a market value of at least $3 million.

REGIONAL EXCHANGES

There are smaller regional exchanges. Local companies that don't meet the large exhanges' listing requirements typically list here.

TRADING RESTRICTIONS

Drastic moves up or down in the markets could have significant long-term effects on our economy. A variety of mechanisms are in place on U.S. exchanges to prevent large movements up or down. For example, if the Dow Jones Industrial Average moves by 10, 20, and 30% (effective 4/15/98), trading on the NYSE is halted.

IT'S A FACT

The NYSE floor measures about 36,000 square feet.

HOW AN AUCTION MARKET WORKS

U*nderstanding how a trade works in the auction market can help you make better decisions about your own trades.*

◀ OPENING BELL

On the New York Stock Exchange a bell signals the beginning of trading each day. Bells were introduced in the 1870s. First, a Chinese gong was used, but brass bells have been used since the exchange moved to its current location in 1903.

1 YOU PLACE AN ORDER

You decide to buy or sell shares of stock. You call your broker and place the order.

2 YOUR BROKER SENDS THE ORDER

Your broker sends the order to the firm's order room, which sends it immediately to the trading floor of the exchange where the stock trades.

3 YOUR ORDER GOES TO THE POST

Your order is received at the brokerage firm's order booth on the perimeter of the trading floor. It's then electronically routed to the trading post for that stock, and the trade will be completed at the best price available.

For orders over 30,099 shares, trades are handled individually (see 4-7 for more explanation).

4 THE TRADING POST DISPLAYS PRICES

The trading post contains a flat-panel display screen at each post to show current quotes for each stock traded there.

5 THE BROKER TALKS TO THE SPECIALIST

The broker asks the specialist for the pricing. The specialist answers "30 1/8 - 30 3/8 - 500 by 100. Last sale 30 1/4." This is shorthand meaning the highest price someone is willing to pay is 30 1/8 and the lowest price someone is willing to sell at is 30 3/8. The phrase "500 by 100" means that current buyers want a total of 50,000 shares (500 lots of 100) and sellers are offering a total of 10,000 shares (100 lots of 100). The last sale occurred at 30 1/4.

6 THE TRADE IS MADE

Someone's broker says that he's selling 40,000 shares at 30 3/8. Any broker in the crowd can participate in trading, so another broker quickly accepts the offer before the first broker can accept it. If the broker had missed this offer, the next one might have been higher. For example, if you look in the newspaper and see a stock had significant swings between high and low prices that day and a lot of shares traded, you can imagine many floor brokers competing quickly and loudly for trades.

IT'S A FACT

About 3,000 people (specialists, brokers, and support staff) work on the NYSE trading floor. The floor contains 17 trading posts with 340 trading positions.

7 THE TRADE IS REPORTED

The specialist books the trade (enters the buyer, seller, trade price, number of shares, and time of trade). The trade data quickly travels to electronic tickers around the world where virtually anyone can see it. The data is also sent to the brokerage firm's electronic bookkeeping system and updates their records. A written confirmation of the trade is sent by mail (see pg. 37).

CLOSING BELL ▶

Ringing the opening and closing bell is a privilege usually reserved for someone celebrating an event. A company listing with the exchange for the first time, visiting dignitaries, celebrities, and retiring members are often those invited to ring the bell.

THE ELECTRONIC MARKET

*A*n electronic market uses computers to conduct its trading. The Nasdaq is the primary exchange controlling the flow of trades made in the electronic market. There is no actual central physical location where trading occurs.

WHAT IT IS

Where the auction market brings people together face-to-face, the electronic market brings traders together through their computers. With no central physical location, two traders can be thousands of miles apart, looking at the same information on their screens at the same time.

MARKET EFFICIENCY

The term *market efficiency* refers to how quickly stock prices adjust to reflect the latest information. The U.S. market is considered to be a very efficient stock market because of modern telecommunications and the intense focus on stock investing from investors worldwide.

WHO WORKS ON AN ELECTRONIC MARKET?

Like the specialists in an auction market, *market makers* are responsible for keeping an orderly flow of trading in a certain stock. A market maker is usually a brokerage firm that wants to create trading opportunities in a certain stock. This means they constantly list prices of these stocks on their computers so that anyone who wants to buy or sell that stock can see their prices and trade with them.

There can be more than one market maker for each stock, unlike in the auction market, where there is only one person (the specialist) per stock. On electronic markets, there is no limit to how many market makers can offer a stock for trade. There could be one or two, or even 25 or 30. As the name implies, if there are no market makers for a stock at a particular time, there is no market for you to trade that stock.

NASDAQ

The Nasdaq, once called the National Association of Securities Dealers Automated Quotation System, is the largest electronic or *over-the-counter* stock exchange. It is run by the National Association of Securities Dealers (NASD). It handles more than half the stock trading in the United States and lists more companies than the NYSE. Many small companies get their start on Nasdaq.

STOCKS ON THE NASDAQ

See the full list of stocks traded on the Nasdaq by going to www.nasdaq.com/asp/symbols.asp on the Internet. This site will also give you free quotes and charts on your favorite stocks.

AFTER-HOURS TRADING

Most trading takes place in the U.S. stock markets during the hours of 9:30 a.m. Eastern Time and 4:00 p.m. Eastern Time. Some trading is allowed after the traditional markets close and is done through electronic trading systems. Until 1999, after-hours trading was mostly restricted to large quantity trades (*big-block* trading) among professionals and institutions.

One after-hours electronic trading network is run by a firm called Instinet. Instinet's service is strictly for large, professional traders such as brokerage firms, mutual funds, and pension plans. Institutions use the system to trade large blocks of shares directly with each other without using brokers or the exchanges. All traders are anonymous, known only to Instinet who handles all of the administrative aspects.

Many other after-hours exchanges are in development, aimed at equalizing trading between professionals and other investors.

BIG AND GETTING BIGGER

More than half of all equity shares traded in the nation trade on the Nasdaq. It is also the largest stock market in the world in terms of share volume and dollar volume traded. As of January 1999, it listed the securities of 5,068 domestic and foreign companies, more than all other U.S. stock markets combined.

HOW THE ELECTRONIC MARKET WORKS

W*ithout a trading floor, the electronic market exists on computer screens. On the Nasdaq, trading information is simultaneously broadcast to over 500,000 computers worldwide. This gives all participants equal access to the market of stocks traded through Nasdaq.*

PLACING AN ORDER

Ordering stock on an electronic market is basically the same for an investor as it would be on an auction market. The difference is in how the trade is executed.

SMALL ORDERS

Many investors, especially beginners, place orders for less than 1,000 shares. These orders are typically handled on a system called the *Small Order Execution System (SOES)*. This system was designed to guarantee that small orders would be automatically executed at the best possible price available on Nasdaq.

AFTER THE ORDER IS PLACED

The SOES system automatically directs the order to the market maker offering the best price to complete the order. It is programmed to guarantee that you will receive the *best displayed price* offered when your order is entered. All market makers in the Nasdaq National Market system are required to route orders for 1,000 shares or less through this system.

7 The SOES ensures fair treatment for certain market orders up to 1,000 shares.

INSIDE MARKET

The *inside market* is the term used to describe the highest price at which you can sell a stock and the lowest price at which you can buy a stock.

CROSSING MARKETS

Many of the after-hours trading firms only *cross* trade. This means, that they will match a buy order with a sell order if they have been entered at the same price.

WHAT STOCKS CAN BE LISTED ON NASDAQ?

To be listed on the Nasdaq, common and preferred stock must have a minimum bid price of $1. Nasdaq says that this requirement provides a safeguard against certain market activity associated with low-priced securities, and also enhances the overall credibility of the market. Nasdaq is the only market that has a stated minimum bid price requirement.

AFTER-HOURS TRADES

The after-hours market for stock trading is making a lot of news, but it's still in its infancy. It may make trading by individual investors a lot riskier than trading on an established exchange during normal trading hours. For example:

- Trading isn't reported as part of the closing prices in newspapers. If news about a company emerges after hours, the opening price the next day may be far different than the previous day's closing price, and you would have no way of knowing that information;

- There is no centralized reporting system. You have to track prices and trading volume across all of the after-hours services;

- There is much less trading after hours, so small trades, odd lots and other unusual orders may be harder to fill;

- With fewer people trading, that same news might create a pent-up demand waiting to be filled until normal hours, or a panic waiting to explode when normal trading hours resume;

- Trading virtually around the clock leaves little time for decisions based on reflection and research.

HOW A TRADE WORKS

U*nlike most markets where people buy and sell products, in the stock market, buyers buy at different prices than sellers sell.*

WHEN YOU BUY: THE ASK

When you want to buy a stock, you look at a quote called the *ask*. Buyers always pay the ask, which is always higher than the bid. For example, if the ask for a stock is $40, you would pay $4,000 for 100 shares.

PLUS COMMISSION

The brokerage commission is added to the purchase cost. If the commission is $15, you would pay $4,015 to own the 100 shares of stock. This total amount is what you report to the IRS as the cost of your investment.

THE SPREAD

Why are buying and selling prices different? It's because of the *spread*—the profit for the market makers. They make their living by taking a cut of each transaction. If no one else wants shares at a certain price, they may buy the shares for their own account, becoming investors who can make or lose money just like any other investor.

WHEN YOU SELL: THE BID

The price at which you can sell your stock, is called the *bid*. Sellers always receive the bid as their selling price, which is always lower than the ask. For example, if the ask for a stock is $40, the bid might be $39 3/4. In short, you could sell your 100 shares of stock at $39 3/4, or $39.75. That would give you $3,975.

LESS COMMISSION

The brokerage commission is deducted from the proceeds of the sale. If the commission is $15, it would be deducted from the $3,975, leaving you with $3,960. This is the amount you would report to the IRS as the net proceeds from your trade. Notice that if you buy, then quickly sell a stock without the price changing, you will lose money. In this case, $55 ($4,015 - $3,960).

NO BROKER REQUIRED

In most cases, you don't need a broker to trade stock. You can call a company's investor relations department and ask for the name of their *transfer agent* (who issues stock certificates and tracks who owns the stock). This is not an easy way to trade. It's time consuming and may end up costing more than using a broker.

THE SPECIALIST ▶
The specialist "books" each trade and keeps track of all buy and sell orders.

8 Invest a hypothetical $100,000 using The Stock Market Game™ at www.smgww.org.

BROKERS AS INVESTORS

Brokerage firms don't just help you trade. They invest in stocks to make profits, too. Your brokerage firm probably employs individuals, called *traders*, to trade stocks for the firm's own account. Sometimes the firm will fill your order by selling shares from their own account (or buying them for their own account) rather than sending the trade through to an exchange. In this way, the firm lowers the cost of the transaction, avoiding the spread and exchange fees.

PLACING ORDERS

K nowing the kind of trade you want to make, its purpose, and the proper terminology are crucial, because once you give instructions for a trade, it's live until subsequent instructions are given that amend or cancel your first instructions, which by then, may be too late.

THE PURPOSE

There are strategies to trading and different kinds of orders to help you conduct those strategies. Some are price-sensitive. Others are time-sensitive. You can also combine types of orders to achieve even more precise objectives.

Market order. Also called buying or selling *at the market*, this order tells the broker to buy or sell it now, whatever the market price.

Day order. A day order is cancelled if it isn't *executed* (completed) by the close of trading on the same day it's placed.

Good 'til cancelled order (GTC). A GTC order stays open until it's executed or until you call your broker and cancel it. Some brokers restrict the length of time a GTC can remain open to "end of same month" or "no more than 30 days."

Limit order. Investors can protect themselves from paying too much or selling for too little by using a limit order. The trade may not occur, but if it does, you're guaranteed that price or better. For example, if you want to buy a stock if it drops to $30, you can place a limit order to buy for no more than $30. If the price falls to $30, the broker will attempt to buy it. If someone else buys it first and the price immediately rises, you will miss out. Similarly, you might want to sell your stock if it rises to $40, so you place a limit order to sell, but at no less than $40.

Stop-loss order. What if you have a profit and are afraid of losing it if the price suddenly drops? You can place a stop-loss order that's designed to stop a loss. For example, if you bought a stock at $10 and it's now $30, you might place a stop-loss order to sell if the price drops to $20. If the next trade after it hits $20 is 19 1/2, then you would sell at 19 1/2.

ROUND LOTS AND ODD LOTS ▶

Buying and selling in round lots is the most common way stocks trade. A round lot is equal to 100 shares. Buying or selling an odd lot means you're trading an amount other than a multiple of 100. The main disadvantage of an odd lot trade is that your price may be slightly higher to compensate for breaking up a round lot. On the other hand, many investors who want to own a stock but don't have enough money to buy 100 shares, consider owning fewer shares to be worth the extra cost.

NO NASDAQ STOP LOSSES

Nasdaq does not officially accept stop loss orders since each market maker sets its own prices. Many brokers will set stop-loss orders on their own systems and then enter the order on the Nasdaq if the stop-loss price is reached.

BOTTOM FISHING

You're a bottom fisher if you're looking to buy stock that's going down or has already suffered drastic price declines. In other words, you are looking for a bargain stock to buy that has hit bottom.

SELLING STOCK YOU DON'T OWN

You can actually sell a stock without owning it first. This is called *shorting* the stock, *selling short*, or conducting a *short sale*. Here's how shorting a stock works.

You borrow the stock from your brokerage firm then sell it in the market just as if you owned it, subject to a few trading restrictions. You hope that the stock's price falls so you can buy the stock at a lower price and keep the difference as your profit.

If the price rises, you will either have to buy the stock at the higher price and take a loss, or wait for the price to fall again. The higher the price goes, however, the more you can lose—the sky's the limit.

WORKING WITH A BROKER

Setting up and managing your account can be as important as making the right investment decisions.

TYPES OF ACCOUNTS

*I*f you want to trade stocks through a broker, you need to open an account. Different types of accounts give you different opportunities. Each represents a different level of risk and of your creditworthiness as judged by the brokerage firm.

CASH ACCOUNT

This is the traditional brokerage account. If you have a cash account, you pay in full for all purchases by the settlement date, which, for stocks, is three days. This is becoming less common in the age of Internet trading. Most brokers require the money to be in your account before they will accept an order to buy. Just about anyone can open a cash account, although some brokerage firms may require a significant deposit (e.g., $10,000) before they will open the account.

MARGIN ACCOUNT

This type of account allows you to borrow money based on the value of the *marginable* securities you own. Marginable securities are those that the broker and regulators consider to be worthy of acting as security in case you don't repay the loan. Because the brokerage firm is essentially granting you credit by letting you open a margin account, you must pass their screening procedure to get one.

UPSIDE/DOWNSIDE: MARGIN ACCOUNTS

Upside. You can borrow at lower interest rates than generally available elsewhere, get cash from your stock without paying taxes or losing the opportunity for the price to rise, or use the money to buy more securities or even for non-investing purposes.

Downside. Interest mounts the longer you borrow. If the value of the securities backing the loan drops below a certain amount, your broker will ask you to deposit more money in the account to cover the lost amount. If you don't add more money, the broker can sell your stocks to recoup the loan amount. In short, there's the potential to lose much more than you borrow.

OTHER FEES

Ask about fees to transfer assets out of your account, inactive account fees, minimums for interest on non-margin cash balances, annual IRA custodial fees, per-transaction charges, margin interest rates, or other fees specific to your needs.

OPTION ACCOUNT

This type of account allows you to trade stock options. To open this type of account, your broker will require you to sign a statement that you understand and acknowledge the risks associated with these types of investments. The agreement came into existence after clients who experienced large losses in options successfully sued brokers by claiming they were unaware of the risks. Be sure that you also receive a brochure explaining the risks and rewards of options trading.

THINGS TO KNOW

- You will almost certainly have a bit of cash in a brokerage account of any type, perhaps because you received a dividend payment. This cash balance may be carried along as pure cash (and you get no interest), or the cash may be swept into a money market account (so you get some interest).

- If you want to transfer your account to another broker, you fill out an Automated Customer Account Transfer (ACAT) form through your new broker. The new broker will generally require a copy of your statements from the old brokerage house, plus some additional proof of identity. The transfer will be made within 5-10 business days for regular accounts, and 10-15 business days for IRA and other types of retirement accounts. The paperwork starts the process, but thereafter it's all done electronically. Some brokerage firms charge fees as high as $50 to close IRA accounts. Others will reimburse a portion to cover those fees. Be sure to ask.

STOCKBROKERS AND BROKERAGE FIRMS

C hoosing the right stockbroker can make your investment decisions easier and perhaps more profitable.

WHO IS A STOCKBROKER?

Stockbrokers, also known as registered representatives, have passed strict tests to become licensed to buy and sell stocks for their clients. Typically, they split the commission from trades with their brokerage firm. Each brokerage firm may have its own name to identify their brokers. For example, your broker might be called a Financial Representative, Investment Advisor, or another name, depending on what the brokerage firm decided would sound best.

CHOOSING A BROKER

Different brokers have different investment philosophies and strategies. It's important to find one who takes your needs, goals, and risk concerns into consideration before taking any money from you. A broker who doesn't have your best interests in mind may lead you into investments that won't help you achieve your goals, or that make you uncomfortable because you don't understand them.

FULL SERVICE

A full service broker can take orders for any trades you wish to make. Their commissions are usually higher than discount brokerage firms, because they need to cover the cost of more services. People use full service brokers because they may not want to do their own research, they want advice on different types of financial, tax or retirement planning, or certain investment options, access to IPOs, they don't have the time to spend trading stocks, or just prefer the experience of a professional.

BROKER

The term was first used around 1622 to mean an agent in financial transactions. Originally, it referred to wine retailers—those who broach (break) wine casks.

TRADING WITH DISCRETION

Discretion means your broker has your permission to trade stocks in your account without asking you first. People who have a lot of trust in their broker might consider giving this right which frees the broker to act quickly on opportunities. Be careful, though. The broker might also sell something you wanted to keep, or invest in ways you find inappropriate.

DISCOUNT

Discount brokerage firms were created as a self service form of securities investing. Commissions were so low because these firms would execute trades exactly as clients requested, and nothing more. Over time, discount brokerages have become more like full service brokerages, offering almost all the services of a full service broker with the exception of giving advice. Many do, however, offer newsletters outlining their investment philosophies.

DEEP DISCOUNT

Deep discount firms began as a no-frills service to undercut discount brokerage prices. The small commission covered the handling of the trade and virtually nothing else. Online brokers, with their relatively low overhead, have changed the equation dramatically. They are the same as deep discount, but are designed mainly for computer users. Some brokerage firms offer online trading that is cheaper than talking to a broker, with lower commissions. Competition among these firms is fierce and rates have dropped as low as $8 per trade. Some require a cash deposit of $10,000, before clients can place trades, protecting them from non-payers.

UPSIDE/DOWNSIDE: TYPES OF BROKERS

Full service. Upside is someone who can give you advice and support, and do the legwork on research and administration. Downside is generally higher fees.

Discount. Upside is a low fee structure, access to information that can help decisions, and no one trying to convince you about opportunities, if you like making your own decisions. Downside is that you're on your own.

Deep discount. Upside is a low fee structure. Downside is no other support.

KEEPING RECORDS

*Y*our broker will send you various documents that are important for tracking your investments and essential for tax preparation.

STATEMENT

Depending upon the type of brokerage account you have, you will receive statements monthly or quarterly. These statements detail all the activity in your account over the time period covered by the statement. Each brokerage firm has a slightly different format, but all generally provide the same information.

PORTFOLIO DETAILS ▼

The portion of your statement shown below tells you what assets were in your account at the end of the statement period. Most statements, like this one, group all the similar assets (all stocks, all bonds, etc.), then list the assets within each group in alphabetical order.

ACCOUNT ACTIVITY

Every statement will show you a detailed, chronological listing of every transaction that occurred during the statement period. By reading this section, you can follow the trail of events that brought your account from its opening value to its closing value. You can also read it to check for errors or mistaken charges that might happen from time to time.

Quantity
How much you own of the asset listed on that line.

Current Price
The price of each unit of your asset as of the last day of the statement period.

Current Value
Multiply the quantity by the current price to see the value of the asset on the day the period ended.

Estimated Accrued Interest
For investments that pay interest, such as bonds, there is an estimate of how much interest you would receive if you sold the investment on the last day of the statement period. The term accrued means that the interest is owed to you even if it hasn't yet been paid into your account.

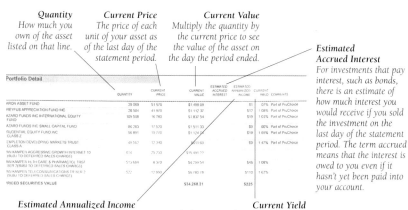

	QUANTITY	CURRENT PRICE	CURRENT VALUE	ESTIMATED ACCRUED INTEREST	ESTIMATED ANNUALIZED INCOME	CURRENT YIELD	COMMENTS
ARON ASSET FUND	29 069	51 570	$1 499 09		$1	07%	Part of ProChoice
REYFUS APPRECIATION FUND INC	26 504	41 970	$1 112 37		$17	1 08%	Part of ProChoice
AZARD FUNDS INC INTERNATIONAL EQUITY FUND	109 508	16 780	$1 837 54		$19	1 03%	Part of ProChoice
AZARD FUNDS INC SMALL CAPITAL FUND	86 263	17 520	$1 511 33		$9	60%	Part of ProChoice
RUCENTIAL EQUITY FUND INC CLASS Z	56 891	19 770	$1 124 14		$19	1 69%	Part of ProChoice
EMPLETON DEVELOPING MARKETS TRUST CLASS A	49 562	12 340	$611 60		$9	1 47%	Part of ProChoice
AN KAMPEN AGGRESSIVE GROWTH INTERNET 10 (BUILT TO DEFERRED SALES CHARGE)	614	25 230	$15 491 22				
AN KAMPEN HEALTH CARE & PHARMACEUT TRIST SER 7 (BUILT TO DEFERRED SALES CHARGE)	513 684	8 370	$4 299 54		$46	1 08%	
AN KAMPEN TELECOMMUNICATIONS TR SER 2 (BUILT TO DEFERRED SALES CHARGE)	527	12 990	$6 780 78		$110	1 62%	
RICED SECURITIES VALUE			$34 268.21		$225		

Estimated Annualized Income
How much your investment is projected to earn for the entire year in interest, dividends, or both.

Current Yield
Divide the estimated annualized income by the current value of the asset to find the current yield as of the close of the statement period.

TRADE CONFIRMATION

After you buy or sell a stock, your broker will send you a confirmation. If you have the money in your account, the confirmation is for your information only. If you don't have the money in your account, the confirmation is your notice to send money to your broker for the amount of the trade plus any commissions. Keep all your confirmations. In case of a dispute, it's your record of the trade. If something isn't correct on the confirmation, notify your broker immediately.

9 Your confirmation and statement are your permanent records of your stock activities.

General Information
This section tells you exactly what you bought or sold, how much you paid and any other necessary information which may affect your trade.

Prospectus Confirmation
Through The Courtesy Of:

ON 01/27/2000 YOU PURCHASED 302.801
MFS SERIES TRUST VI UTILITIES FUND CLB   AT $13.21
TICKER SYMBOL MMUSX

ON SELLING YOUR SHARES, YOU MAY PAY A SALES CHARGE. FOR THE
CHARGE AND OTHER FEES, SEE THE PROSPECTUS, UNSOLICITED
PROSPECTUS ENCLOSED OR TO FOLLOW UNDER SEPARATE COVER

Amount   4,000.00

Net Amount   4,000.00
Due Date   02/01/2000

Costs and Fees
This section details what you paid or received and any fees associated with your trade. It also tells the due date for paying any money you may owe on this trade.

The Bottom Line
The bottom line on your confirmation identifies the trade for the clearinghouse—the organization that handles all the administrative tasks involved in trading.

10 Keep all your statements and other documents in a safe place.

REPORTING DIVIDENDS

By January 31 of each year, all companies, by law, must send a form called a 1099 DIV to each shareholder who has received dividends during the year. The 1099 DIV shows the total amount of dividends paid to the shareholder for the year. The shareholder must report the amount to the IRS. If your broker holds your stock for you, s/he will receive each 1099 DIV and then send you a consolidated one showing the dividend income from all your stock investments. If your dividends are reinvested for you (as in a DRIP), you may avoid paying taxes on any gains until you sell your investment. The dividends themselves, of course, are always taxable.

BUYING AND SELLING

The saying goes that at any given moment, a stock is worth whatever someone is willing to pay for it. There are different methods you can use to determine a stock's value that will make your decisions better and help to minimize your risk of investing.

WAYS TO ANALYZE STOCKS

*M*ost investing is based on future expectations, so most stock analysis focuses on trying to predict future prices. Here are some methods beginners and experts both can use.

FUNDAMENTAL ANALYSIS

Fundamental analysis focuses on factors that can make a company's earnings rise or fall. Analysts study the company and the factors likely to affect it, then try to gauge what the future might bring. For example, in a good economy, people might increase vacations and buy more leisure products. Analysts might, therefore, recommend buying leisure stocks in anticipation of higher sales. Many experts recommend that new investors simply look at the world around them and see which products and companies they like. You can compare a few competitors' profits and debts, whether one has an edge, such as a patent or a strong brand name, and other factors anyone thinking of buying into a business would consider.

▲ ANNUAL REPORTS

Every publicly traded company publishes an annual report similar to the one above from Lucent Technologies. You can also find information online at www.sec.gov/edgarhp/wedgar.htm. Every year, every public company must do an EDGAR filing of information which is open to anyone who wants to review it.

ANALYZING CHARTS

Technical analysis uses past stock price and trading volume information to predict future price movements. It also attempts to predict the right time to buy and sell stocks. All the information used by technical analysts is charted. Technical analysts believe that:

- Chart patterns represent the behavior of those who like investing in a particular stock. Since that group doesn't change quickly, they believe the stock will have similar chart patterns in the future;
- Since many investors don't react quickly to information, the chart can provide some predictive value that technically-oriented investors can use to their advantage;
- Chart patterns appear over and over again. Analysts believe that even if they don't know why the patterns happen, investors shouldn't trade or invest against them;
- Investors tend to swing from overly optimistic to excessively pessimistic and back again. Technical analysis can show these movements in the charts and predict trends.

COMBINED ANALYSIS

Some investors try to analyze stocks from both a fundamental and technical perspective. For example, if a company appears to be entering a strong business cycle, yet its chart suggests it isn't a good time to buy, an investor might delay a purchase decision. On the other hand, the investor might believe that s/he will be buying before the rest of the market catches on, the charts change, and the technical analysts begin to recommend buying the stock.

RESEARCH ANALYSTS

Research analysts are hired by financial firms to analyze the economy, the market, and/or a particular industry. They may use fundamental or technical analysis, or a combination of the two. Because they're paid to make recommendations to the firm's brokers and to large investors, they can have considerable influence on stock prices. If a well-respected analyst recommends buying a stock, it will often drive up the price. Through the Internet you can now read reports on most stocks, even without an account, just by visiting a firm's website. Be aware, though, that by the time you read a report, much of the investment community has already seen it.

INDEPENDENT ANALYSTS

Many online services offer free stock analyses. Many other services sell their analyses over the Internet and charge a fee for newsletter subscriptions. It may be worth the cost to receive a newsletter that shares your investment philosophy and appreciates your level of risk.

ANALYZING THE STOCK ITSELF

*M**any things can make a stock's price go up or down. Prices are driven by our perceptions of the world around us. No one factor is fully responsible for a stock's price. There are, however, a few main factors that typically drive perceptions, that considered together, give investors a realistic picture of a reasonable price. Here are ways to analyze the relationship between the stock price and the company's earnings and balance sheet.*

BY P/E RATIO

The *price-to-earnings ratio (P/E)* is a measure of what investors will pay for a stock based on its current earnings. Dividing the stock price by the current earnings (for the last 12 months) gives you a number that is a *multiple* of what investors believe the stock is worth.

For example, if a company has earned $1.00 and the stock is selling at $10.00, it's said to have a P/E ratio, or a multiple, of 10 ($10 divided by $1 equals 10). If that multiple is high compared to those of its competitors, an investor might consider the stock to be too expensive for the profits the company generates.

If a company has no earnings, there can't be a P/E ratio. The price is based on investors' perceptions of potential future earnings.

 Stock prices are partly based on our perceptions of what a company is worth.

OVERVALUED OR UNDERVALUED

If a company's business appears to be worth more than its stock price, the stock is considered *undervalued*. For example, a stock may be undervalued because investors are focusing on competitors or a different industry and are ignoring the company. You might decide to buy the stock with the expectation that other investors will eventually notice it, begin buying shares, and drive up the price. If a stock price appears too high in relation to its company's business, the stock is considered *overvalued*. You might decide to sell an overvalued stock expecting that eventually, other investors will notice that the shares are overvalued, sell them, and drive down the price.

BY COMPANY VALUE

If a business sold all its assets and paid all its debts today, what value would be left to share among the owners (the shareholders)? The money each shareholder would receive is called the *book value*, the most basic way to look at a company's worth. For example, if the owners of 10 million shares would split $10 million, the book value of one share would be $1.

Typically, investors are willing to pay more than book value for a company's stock, so analysts will refer to a stock as trading "X times" its book value. The higher the multiple, the more cautious analysts become about future price increases.

ANALYSTS' EXPECTATIONS

A stock's price can go down even if the company does well. For example, when analysts post their expected earnings for a company, many people buy or sell based on those educated predictions. Then, when the actual earnings are announced, investors might:

- Buy because earnings were as good or better than expected;
- Sell because they've made a profit and think the stock may stop rising;
- Sell because earnings failed to meet analysts' expectations.

BY YIELD

If a company distributes some of its earnings to shareholders as dividends, there are tangible immediate earnings for investors, rather than the potential of earnings from a price increase. These earnings are a stock's *yield*. The higher a stock's yield, the more attractive it will be to investors.

To calculate a stock's yield, divide the total annual dividend by the stock price. For example, if a stock pays $1 in dividends per year and is trading at $10, its yield is 10%.

BY EARNINGS PER SHARE

Companies announce their earnings every three months. The amount reported is a per-share amount. If a company announces earnings of 25¢ and they have 10 million shares outstanding, it means they earned a total of $2,500,000.

Earnings per share (EPS) is the best measure of how a company is performing. Steady earnings increases indicate that a company is doing well and should be reflected in the stock price. Erratic or reduced earnings may indicate that the company is having troubles and should also show up in the stock price. However, unstable earnings might also be an indication that the company is reorganizing, pointing to positive earnings potential in the future.

ANALYZING THE BUSINESS CLIMATE

*P*eople who analyze stocks based on business performance try to
see into the future to spot issues that could ripple through to the
company, and ultimately, its stock price.

NATIONAL ECONOMY

The general economic climate has a major impact on stock prices. If the economy is doing well, that means business in general is doing well, and vice versa. Analysts constantly eye statistical trends that help them gauge the overall health of the economy. Here are a few examples:

- **Interest rates.** If they go up, they could make money harder to borrow and inhibit business growth—unless investors think higher rates will help business by slowing it just enough to help keep the rate of inflation in check;
- **Unemployment.** If people are employed, they have money to spend. That may be good for business,unless investors think that with so many people employed there may be too much money being spent and the rising demand for products might cause inflation;
- **Housing starts.** Increases in new home building signals optimistic consumers. It also means that all the businesses involved in new homes, from copper and wood to home furnishings, should benefit.

THE SECTOR

A sector is a segment of the economy that may encompass many industries. Investment professionals analyze the business prospects of the sector of the economy in which a business operates. For example, they may evaluate the high technology sector when analyzing a company in the software industry.

12 If you are a long-term investor and think a company is strong, temporary swings in the economy or the market become less important.

13 Every sales piece is required to tell you that past performance is no guarantee of future success.

14 Stock prices are often affected by interest rate announcements from the Federal Reserve.

THE INDUSTRY

It's often possible to see direct links between events that cause changes to an entire industry and the businesses in that industry. A major research breakthrough, for example, might boost every business in a particular industry.

Investment professionals also tend to set statistical boundaries for stock prices within each industry that they become cautious about crossing. For example, investors who follow P/E ratios (see p. 40) may only be willing to pay prices between 20 and 30 times earnings for a drug stock because the stocks have typically traded in that range. At the same time, they may be willing to pay thousands of times earnings for an Internet stock because its earnings could explode at any time to spectacular heights.

THE COMPANY

Companies are analyzed inside and out to see how they compare to others in their industry. There are many factors. For example, one company may have:
- Better products or more efficient operations;
- Management that seems to make better decisions;
- A more recognizable brand name and more loyal customers.

Investors may also flock to a company when it introduces a new product that promises to help it outpace the competition.

How Can You Earn Money from Stock?

Put your money in stocks you believe will give you a higher return than you might get elsewhere, taking into consideration how much risk you are willing to accept to make money. Here is what you can expect to earn from your stock ownership.

From Price Appreciation

People buy a stock hoping its price will increase over time. If the company is doing well, shows consistent revenue and earnings increases, and grows at a rate equal to or greater than the economy, its stock price can be expected to *appreciate* (rise). If you buy a stock at $10 and the price goes up to $20, for example, you can sell it and say you have earned $10 on your investment (minus commissions).

By Borrowing Money

Your stock can give you a form of credit which allows you to buy more stock without spending much more money. This strategy is called buying on *margin*, a way of borrowing against the value of stocks you own in order to buy more. This is a risky strategy and may or may not actually earn you money in the end. It all depends upon whether the stocks you buy on margin go up or down, by how much, and over what period of time. Be careful, and ask a financial advisor for assistance before trying it for yourself.

Stock as a Tax "Shelter"

If the stock is held in a retirement plan account, any rise in the stock value whether *realized* (you sold the stock and have a gain from the sale) or *unrealized* (you still own the stock and the gain is only on paper), is not taxed until the funds are withdrawn at retirement. Also, any dividends paid on stocks owned in a retirement account enjoy the same tax deferral.

FROM INCOME

You may earn income when you own a stock. Dividends are paid to shareholders when a company has earnings that it does not need to reinvest into the company, but chooses to distribute to its shareholders.

How do dividends get paid? If the board of directors declares a dividend, it will announce that the dividend will be paid to shareholders of record as of the *record date* and will be paid or distributed on the *distribution date* (sometimes called the *payable date*). In order to be a shareholder of record on the record date you must own the shares on that date (when the books close for that day).

Since virtually all stock trades are settled in three business days, you must buy the shares at least three days before the record date in order to be the shareholder of record on that date. You can sell it the very next day and still get the dividend. Someone who buys the stock on the record date does not get the dividend. A stock paying a $.50 quarterly dividend will trade for $.50 less on that date, all things being equal. In other words, it trades for its previous price, minus the dividend. This is also known as the *ex-dividend date*.

Who receives the dividend? On the distribution date, shareholders of record will get the dividend. If you own the shares yourself, the company will mail you a check. If you participate in a DRIP (Dividend Re-Investment Plan),

and elect to reinvest the dividend, you will have the dividend credited to your DRIP account and shares purchased for you. If your broker is holding the stock for you, the broker will receive the dividend from the company and credit it to your account.

Predicting the dividend before it's declared. Many companies declare regular dividends every quarter. If a company announces that it can no longer guarantee to maintain the dividend, the dividend may drop drastically the next quarter. You could buy a stock right before the dividend is declared and sell it right after the record date. Chasing dividends, however, will cost you commissions.

Temporary problems. Some companies may be temporarily prohibited from paying dividends on their common stock, usually because they've missed payments on their bonds and/or preferred stock.

ADR dividends. ADRs are dependent on fluctuations in the currency market, so they may pay different dividend amounts each time.

 15 Investors who buy on margin can generally accept a higher level of risk.

COMMON STRATEGIES

T iming is very important to successful stock investing. Knowing strategies for when to buy or sell a stock can help you reduce risk and improve returns. While no one can accurately predict the exact right time to buy or sell, these general guidelines can help you make better decisions.

WHEN THE PRICE RISES

You may hope to sell a stock just before the price drops. No one, however, can be sure of a stock's highest price until after it drops. Therefore, it often makes sense to set profit goals or price targets as a more conservative strategy. For example, if a stock's price rises to a price target, you can sell. If the stock continues to rise, you may choose to bypass your goal and watch the stock carefully for signs of a downturn.

Stop-loss orders (see pg. 30) may help you preserve profits and feel more comfortable about trying to guess price trends. If you own a stock that has gone from $10 to $30, for example, you might place a stop-loss order at $25 to assure a good profit. If the stock continues to rise, you could cancel the stop-loss order and place a new one one at a higher price.

WHEN THE PRICE DROPS

When a stock price drops, should you sell it or buy more? It might be a good time to sell, if you have a profit and are unsure of the stock's future. Before buying more shares, you may want to follow the advice of many experts who suggest waiting for a stock to first demonstrate that it has quit going down. Rarely do stocks have a big decline and a big move back up within a few days. A full service broker can offer advice. If you use a discount broker, you're on your own.

> **16** If your circumstances change, you should review your stock investment strategies.

WHEN THERE'S GOOD NEWS

You heard something good about a company on the news. Everyone else heard the news too and it may already have caused the stock price to go up. If you believe the future of the company looks very promising and the stock will continue to rise, then it might be a good time to buy. If, however, the stock has risen dramatically on the good news, you might want to wait first to see if the price drops back down a little.

17 A long-term holding strategy will eliminate the need for you to watch your stock daily.

WHEN THERE'S BAD NEWS

If one piece of bad news gets out, investors may fear there will be more. Similarly, if one stock in a group hits trouble, there may be a suspicion that others will follow. Watching the news carefully and evaluating your moves based on your own goals may prevent you from flipflopping with the crowd. Just because your stock went down on bad news today doesn't mean it won't rebound tomorrow.

WHEN THE MARKET IS TOO HIGH OR LOW

If the market has risen significantly and you're worried it may be due for a *correction* you might want to place stop-loss orders on your stocks to preserve profits, sell off some of your stocks to secure your profits and reduce your exposure to losses, or delay any new purchases. If you think the market is too low, you might want to buy more stock at these bargain prices.

WHEN A GROUP IS HIGH OR LOW

You may be able to locate a group of similar stocks that are rising and find good companies within the group that haven't yet risen. Sometimes when the *best* companies in a group have been bid up to full value investors will settle for the next best companies and bid up their prices, as well.

COMMON RISKS

*E*very investment has risks. The most important thing to know about risk, however, is that its relevance really depends on your situation. Although every stock can encounter problems, they could have little effect on your situation while having great impact on someone else's situation.

VOLATILITY

Volatility is the risk that comes to virtually everyone's mind when considering investing. If a stock is *volatile*, its price has a tendency to rise and fall dramatically. If a stock is *stable*, investors anticipate its price will fluctuate within small ranges. Investors who need to preserve their cash, or who may unexpectedly need to sell their shares to raise cash, tend to shy away from volatile stocks.

On the other hand, stocks as a whole have historically been the best performing investments over any ten-year period. For people with long-term goals, therefore, stocks are usually considered the most likely investments to help them achieve those goals.

INDUSTRY RISK

Investing in particular industries can increase or decrease your risk. Utilities have traditionally been a relatively low risk industry. Everyone uses heat, water, and power no matter what the economy or the world is doing. Utility stocks also tend to pay consistent dividends, which also lowers volatility.

Internet stocks tend to be high risk because competition is so fierce and investor loyalty can be fickle. In an industry where profits and losses can both be great, these investments are usually highly speculative.

In short, each industry poses its own set of investment risks. The strength of each company within the industry will raise or lower those risks.

18 A stock that's risky for someone else may not be risky for you. Risk is best viewed in relation to your goals, strategy, and time frame.

MARKET RISK

The stock market as a whole—not just your stock—can be quite volatile. The announcement of an interest rate rise can lead investors to think that higher borrowing costs will restrict business growth and send the stock market prices lower. Consequently, if the market drops, your stocks might follow even if the companies are doing well. It's wise, therefore, to evaluate the market environment in addition to your stocks, in order to manage risk.

 19 Determining your level of risk is crucial to successful stock investing.

FOREIGN RISK

Investing in markets outside your own country carries added risks. To invest overseas, you must exchange your dollars for the currency of the other country, then make your purchase. If the value of that currency drops in relation to the dollar, your stock will be worth less in dollars even if the stock price stays the same. On the other hand, if the currency rises in value, you could profit even without the stock price changing. The volatility of the currency and foreign markets may further increase risk. For example, you might have large gains but lose them when you exchange the foreign currency back into U.S. dollars.

Other risks may include the potential for problems with the foreign government or economy that might lead to market declines or make retrieiving your money difficult. Investing in ADRs can reduce this risk.

INFLATION RISK

If the inflation rate is above zero, then your money loses some purchasing power every year. If you invest in stocks that don't increase in value at an equal or faster pace than inflation, you will be losing value, even if it looks like the stock price is going up.

20 Putting your money in a savings account rather than investing in stocks may pose a risk if your goals require investing for a greater return.

TAXES

Understanding some tax basics can help reduce your tax burden and keep more of the money you've worked hard to earn. As much as any other aspect of investing, your tax situation is individual. Check with your tax advisor for more complete explanations.

WHAT'S TAXABLE?

Only a *net profit* is taxable. A net profit is the gain after deducting commissions or fees.

Unrealized gains. When a stock price rises higher than your original purchase price plus any fees you paid, you have a gain. But until you sell, the gain is *unrealized*—it's only on paper (your statement).

Realized gains. Once you sell a stock at a profit, that profit becomes a *realized* gain—you actually have the profit in your account.

Dividends. The dividends you receive are considered income, similar to being paid a salary at a job. Dividends owed to you which you haven't yet received are called *accrued dividends*.

PUT IT AWAY AND DON'T LOOK

Many investors buy a stock with the intention of holding it for years, watching the price rise, and seeing their money grow. They don't bother watching the short-term ups and downs. They also don't have to report any gains to the IRS until they sell their investment.

- If you've bought shares of a particular stock over time at various prices, selling the less profitable shares is a method of reducing the amount of taxes you pay on your capital gains (at the time of the trade you indicate which shares you're selling). Keeping good records of how many shares you bought and when you bought them can help you reduce your tax burden.

- Keep all copies of your trade confirmation reports, statements, and company DRIP (Dividend Re-Investment Program) statements. When figuring gains and losses, be careful not to pay the IRS twice. Some investors who participate in DRIPs forget about the taxes they've already paid on their reinvested dividends and pay again on their tax returns.

- Various costs and fees related to investing may be tax deductible. This may include items such as margin interest, subscriptions, cable TV, phone calls with your investment advisor, and other investment related activities.

21 Keeping good records can help you make decisions that could reduce your tax liabilities.

TIME AFFECTS TAXES

The tax rate used to calculate tax on the net profit from a stock sale varies based on how long you've owned the stock.

Less than a year. *Short-term capital gains* are profits from the sale of stock owned less than a year. You're taxed at your usual income tax rate, unless the profit pushes you into a new income tax bracket.

More than a year. *Long-term capital gains* are profits from selling stock you've owned for more than a year. These are taxed at a rate that's lower than most people's income tax rate.

THE EFFECT OF LOSSES

Losses are tax deductible. You may deduct up to $3,000 in net capital losses each year. Additional losses can be carried forward to the next year. For example, if you made $5,000 in capital gains and sold other stock for $10,000 in capital losses, you could match the $5,000 gain with $5,000 of loss and have zero taxable profits. You would also be allowed to deduct another $3,000 of your loss against your income on your taxes for the year. The remaining $2,000 would carry over to the next tax year, where you could deduct or use it to match up against $2,000 of new capital gains.

SPECIAL TAX SITUATIONS

H ere are some special tax situations you might consider. Again, as much as any other aspect of investing, your tax situation is individual. Check with your tax advisor for more complete explanations.

DEFERRING TAXES

The money you contribute to an IRA, 401(k) account, or Keogh plan is usually—but not always—tax deductible. The amount you contribute may directly reduce your annual taxable income.

WASH SALES

Years ago, investors would sell shares that had gone down in price, take the loss for tax purposes, then quickly buy back the same shares at roughly the same price. This strategy would allow them to get a tax break and still have their stock. Today, that practice is called a *wash sale*, and the IRS doesn't permit you to do it.

In order to take a loss on a stock, you must avoid selling the shares and buying "substantially the same shares" (IRS terminology) within 30 days of each other. If you do, the IRS will disallow the loss and actually add the amount of that loss to the cost basis of the stock you buy. For a definition of what constitutes "substantially the same shares," contact your tax advisor.

 22 A DRIP account is one way a minor can own stocks.

DRIPS

DRIP stands for *Dividend (or Direct) Re-Investment Plan*. This program allows an investor to buy shares of a company without paying any commission. Typically, all the money from dividends is immediately used to purchase more of the same shares. In other words, the dividends are reinvested.

Most plans allow investors to purchase additional shares directly from the company every quarter. This helps make DRIPs an easy, low-cost way of buying common stocks. They are also a convenient way to invest a small amount in a stock each month. A common use of a DRIP is to give a small amount of stock as a gift and let the shares grow through automatic reinvestment.

THINGS TO KNOW

- If the IRS considers you a bad risk because you've underpaid taxes or been negligent in filing, they will ask you to pay *backup withholding*. If this is your situation, your broker is required to withhold (and send to the IRS) 31% of the proceeds of any transaction (on the assumption that the entire amount is a taxable gain). You will get back any excess over your actual tax liability once the IRS completes its review of your file.

- If you have shares that have become worthless, you may deduct the full cost of those shares when you do your taxes. The most important piece of information the IRS wants to know, is what year the shares became worthless.

- Don't confuse a bankrupt company with one that's out of business. Many companies continue operating while in bankruptcy proceedings and their stocks continue to trade. So the stock, by definition, is not worthless. In fact, sometimes *turnaround specialists* buy bankrupt companies, turn around their businesses, and produce vital companies with stocks worth keeping.

GIFTING STOCK

If you give someone shares of stock as a gift, there may be tax implications. You can transfer a gain but not a loss to another individual. Check with your tax advisor if you plan on giving away any stock.

23

Once a child reaches majority age, s/he can use the money in an UGMA for any purpose—whether you like it or not (see the little devil below).

KIDS WITH STOCK

The *Uniform Gifts to Minors Act (UGMA)* is a way for a minor to own securities. An UGMA account is a trust account you can set up at any financial institution without an attorney.

No contracts. In most states, minors can't be bound by a contract. If a broker takes a minor's account, the minor, upon reaching majority, could repudiate any losing trades and force the broker to take the losses. UGMA provides a legal way around this issue.

Children may pay taxes. The income from an UGMA account may be taxable. Assuming the child has no other income and is under age 14, the first $700 is tax-free. The next $700 is taxed at 15%, and the rest is taxed at the parents' top bracket. Once a child becomes 14, all the income is recorded on the child's return at the child's income tax rate.

INFORMATION EVERYWHERE

Information is your most valuable resource when investing in stocks. New information is constantly entering the market. An investor always needs to be listening for new information.

FINDING RELIABLE SOURCES

*L*istening *to the opinions of others can be valuable. At some point, though, every investor has to make a decision, trust his or her own reasoning, and take responsibility for the outcome—good or bad.*

INVESTING VERSUS GAMBLING

Many people equate stock investing with gambling. The difference, however, between casinos and stocks is information. With gambling you're dependent on the odds of the game. With stocks, you can gauge your risk before investing and use information to help manage that risk or even turn it to your advantage.

COMPANY REPORTS

The trend has been to make annual reports much friendlier to read. These reports can yield insights into a company's future prospects.

STOCKBROKERS

Stockbrokers are in business to sell you stock, although your success is their success. A critical part of their job is to funnel useful information to you from sources they consider reliable.

TV, MAGAZINES, AND NEWSPAPERS

Newspapers and television can give you a variety of current information. Magazines are most appropriate for information that isn't time-sensitive.

NEWSLETTERS

Information from independent sources can help you make smart decisions. Know who's written the newsletter. They may have hidden agendas for supporting—or trashing—a stock.

ONLINE SERVICES

The Internet has made accessing and using information infinitely easier than ever before. Most online services offer financial news and other detailed financial data. There are also an abundance of individual websites dedicated to investing.

HOT TIPS

These are probably the least reliable and riskiest ways of getting information. Information about a company from someone who works for that company is insider information. If you use it to trade that stock, you may be committing a crime.

THE POWER OF NEWS

News is the most volatile variable of stock investing because it covers everything going on in the world. A company's earnings, industry mergers, non-market news (whether political, social, economic, the weather, or virtually any news of any kind) can affect a stock price. For example, if a building materials company announces worse earnings than expected, its stock price might be expected to fall. But if a major hurricane destroys homes in the company's area, investors might begin speculating in stocks of building materials companies causing the stock's price to rise instead.

TRACKING STOCKS IN THE NEWSPAPERS

Stock prices from the previous day's trading are printed in tables in most newspapers Tuesday through Saturday. The full week's activity is commonly summarized on Sunday. Here are samples of stock tables you might see in your newspaper.

Yld.
This is the current yield of the dividend, which is calculated by dividing the stock's current price into the dividend. For example, the dividend of 48¢ will give you a 1.8% return on your investment.

Div.
This is the annual dividend that will be paid by that particular stock.

Stock
This is an abbreviation of the company's name, because the whole name usually doesn't fit. When you buy a stock, ask your broker for the abbreviation you will find in the newspaper.

52 Week High and Low
These are the highest and lowest prices recorded for that stock over the last 52 weeks.

pf
This indicates that this is a preferred stock.

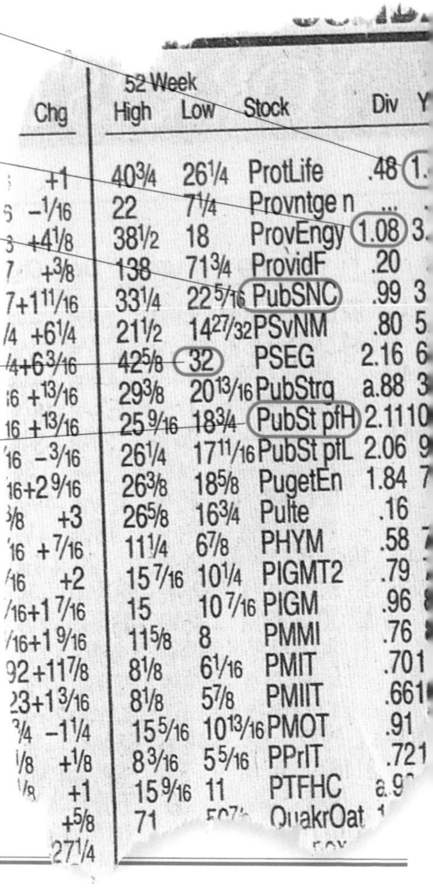

		52 Week				
Chg		High	Low	Stock	Div	Y
+1		40¾	26¼	ProtLife	.48	1.
−¹/₁₆		22	7¼	Provntge n	...	
+4⅛		38½	18	ProvEngy	1.08	3.
+⅜		138	71¾	ProvidF	.20	
+1¹¹/₁₆		33¼	22⁵/₁₆	PubSNC	.99	3
+6¼		21½	14²⁷/₃₂	PSvNM	.80	5
+6³/₁₆		42⅝	32	PSEG	2.16	6
+¹³/₁₆		29⅜	20¹³/₁₆	PubStrg	a.88	3
+¹³/₁₆		25⁹/₁₆	18¾	PubSt pfH	2.1110	
−³/₁₆		26¼	17¹¹/₁₆	PubSt pfL	2.06	9
+2⁹/₁₆		26⅜	18⅝	PugetEn	1.84	7
+3		26⅝	16¾	Pulte	.16	
+⁷/₁₆		11¼	6⅞	PHYM	.58	
+2		15⁷/₁₆	10¼	PIGMT2	.79	
+1⁷/₁₆		15	10⁷/₁₆	PIGM	.96	
+1⁹/₁₆		11⅝	8	PMMI	.76	
+11⅞		8⅛	6¹/₁₆	PMIT	.701	
+1³/₁₆		8⅛	5⅞	PMIIT	.661	
−1¼		15⁵/₁₆	10¹³/₁₆	PMOT	.91	
+⅛		8³/₁₆	5⁵/₁₆	PPrIT	.721	
+1		15⁹/₁₆	11	PTFHC	a.9	
+⅝		71	50⁷·	QuakrOat	1	
27¼						

FOOTNOTES, LEGENDS, AND EXPLANATIONS

Check out your newspaper's footnotes or legend for a detailed explanation of the column headings and symbols. The most commonly used symbols, which explain trading activity are universal among newspapers, but many other explanations vary between newspapers.

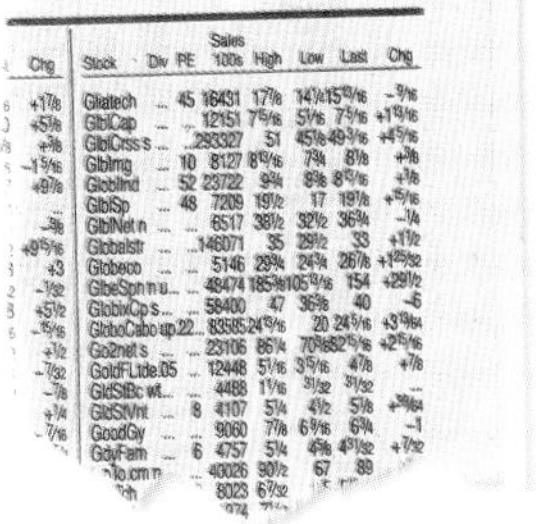

◀ **NASDAQ TABLE**

The information you will find on the Nasdaq table is very similar to the information in the New York Stock Exchange listing detailed below.

PE
This is the price-to-earnings ratio (see page 40).

OTHER ABBREVIATIONS

Abbreviations may vary from your newspaper, but here is some other useful information you may find in a stock listing:

● New 52-week high;
● New 52-week low;
● Extra dividend;
● A P/E equal to or greater than 100;
● A new price reflecting a stock split;
● A new issue within the past 52 weeks;
● X-Dividend (owners of record receive a dividend);
● Trading halted;
● Company in bankruptcy;
● Initial dividend.

Sales 100s	High	Low	Last	Chg
12351	28	26½	27⁵⁄₁₆	+⁹⁄₁₆
5013	9	7¾	8⁷⁄₁₆	−⁹⁄₁₆
1112	36½	35¾	36⁷⁄₁₆	+⁹⁄₁₆
294838	43⅜	78¼	78⁵⁄₁₆	−3¾
10025	33	32⁷⁄₁₆	32¹¹⁄₁₆	+³⁄₁₆
9327	16½	15⅜	15¾	+⁵⁄₁₆
2257	34¾	33⁵⁄₁₆	33¹¹⁄₁₆	+³⁄₁₆
8908	23⅛	22⅝	22⅞	+¼
299	21⅜	21⅛	21³⁄₁₆	−⅛
130721	13⁄₁₆	20⅝	21⅝	+¹⁄₁₆
112744	24⅛	22¹⁄₁₆	23¼	+1⅛
42111617	⁵⁄₁₆	16¹⁵⁄₁₆	17¼	−½
18727	11⁄₁₆	7⅜	7¹¹⁄₁₆	+¼
1371	11¼	10¹⁵⁄₁₆	11⅛	+³⁄₁₆
1764	11⅝	11¹⁄₁₆	11⅝	+½
4022	9½	9⅛	9⁵⁄₁₆	+¹⁄₁₆
7513	6⅜	6⅛	6⁵⁄₁₆	+³⁄₁₆
10006	6¼	6¹⁄₁₆	6³⁄₁₆	+⅛
118411	¹⁵⁄₁₆	11⅝	11¹³⁄₁₆	+⅛
135046	3⁄₁₆	5¹⁵⁄₁₆	6⅛	+¹⁄₁₆
1284	12	11⅝	12	+⁵⁄₁₆
103597	⅞	55¹⁄₁₆	57⅜	+¹³⁄
22	¹⁵⁄₁₆	21³⁄₁₆	21⁹⁄₁	
		32⁷⁄₁₆		
		9¼		

Sales
This is how many shares traded on that particular day. The number given is in "100s." For example, if it listed 5, it would mean 500 shares traded that day.

Last
This is the last or closing price recorded for that day.

Low
This is the lowest price recorded for that day.

Chg.
This is the total change in price from the previous day's closing.

High
This is the highest price recorded for that day.

READING OTHER USEFUL TABLES

There are other sources of important information. For example, the NYSE and Nasdaq both provide tables listing important events from the previous day's trading.

DIARY

This common table recaps the day with overall market data. It encompasses all transactions on that exchange for that trading day.

Advanced, Declined, and Unchanged
These tell how many stocks' prices went up, how many went down, and how many stayed unchanged for that trading day. "Total" shows the number of different stocks that were traded that day.

These numbers tell what direction the overall market went that day. If advances were more than declines, the market is moving in a positive direction, and vice versa. This must be viewed, however, over time, as one day's statistics are not a solid indication of market trends.

Up Volume, Down Volume, and Total Volume
These show the total number of shares that traded higher and traded lower, and the total number of shares traded on the exchange, including those that remained unchanged.

Looking at these figures over time may give you an indication of whether investors are keeping their money in stocks or moving it elsewhere, such as bonds.

Most Active
These are the stocks that traded the most shares. It lists the total number of shares traded, the closing price, and the overall change in the stocks listed.

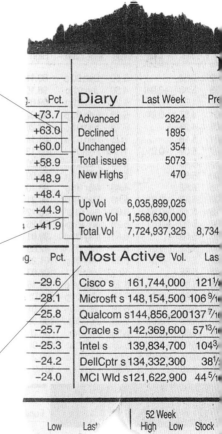

	Pct.	Diary	Last Week	Pre
	+73.7	Advanced	2824	
	+63.0	Declined	1895	
	+60.0	Unchanged	354	
	+58.9	Total issues	5073	
	+48.9	New Highs	470	
	+48.4			
	+44.9	Up Vol	6,035,899,025	
	+41.9	Down Vol	1,568,630,000	
		Total Vol	7,724,937,325	8,734

g.	Pct.	Most Active	Vol.	Las
	−29.6	Cisco s	161,744,000	121¹/
	−28.1	Microsft s	148,154,500	106 ⁹/₁
	−25.8	Qualcom s	144,856,200	137 ⁷/₁
	−25.7	Oracle s	142,369,600	57¹³/₁
	−25.3	Intel s	139,834,700	104³/
	−24.2	DellCptr s	134,332,300	38¹/
	−24.0	MCI Wld s	121,622,900	44 ⁵/₁

			52 Week		
Low	Las'		High	Low	Stock

A BROADER INDICATION

Reading the Diary for a particular exchange will give you the broadest indication of that day's trading activity. Though you may hear that the "Dow" (Dow Jones Industrial Average) went down, advances may have been greater than declines, meaning the overall market actually moved in a positive direction.

NYSE MARKET ▼ RECAP

There is also a market recap for stocks trading on the New York Stock Exchange. The information you will find there is similar, if not identical, to the information displayed on the Nasdaq table.

SDAQ

Gainers	Last	Chg.	Pct.
Conolog n	u5^{11}/$_{16}$	+5^1/$_{32}$	+766.7
Metrocall	u11^5/$_8$	+9^1/$_2$	+447.1
AndrGr	u17^1/$_8$	+11	+179.6
PhrmPrt n	2^{11}/$_{16}$	+1^{21}/$_{32}$	+160.6
PacA&E	u3^{11}/$_{16}$	+2^1/$_4$	+156.5
AmrXtal	u38	+22^{15}/$_{16}$	+152.3
AquisCom	3^{25}/$_{32}$	+2^1/$_4$	+146.9
Firetct	u4	+2^9/$_{32}$	+132.7

Losers	Last	Chg.	Pct.
VirtIC un	5^1/$_4$	-2^3/$_4$	-34.4
ICHOR	2	-1^1/$_8$	-36.0
Vion wtB	4^1/$_8$	-2^5/$_{16}$	-35.9
PlayBy	2^5/$_{16}$	-1^3/$_{16}$	-33.9
Vicor	23^7/$_{32}$	-20^{29}/$_{32}$	-47.4
CentBusn	d4^1/$_2$	-2^3/$_8$	-34.5
SykesEn	d17^{15}/$_{16}$	-9^9/$_{16}$	-34.8

Div   nh   Low   Last   Ch

MARKET SUMMARY F(

NYSE

Diary	Last Week	Prev. Week
Advanced	2193	1329
Declined	1248	2111
Unchanged	228	230
Total issues	3669	3670
New Highs	160	160

Up Vol	3,786,492,694	NA
Down Vol	2,226,526,180	NA
Total Vol	6,225,276,710	6,687,013,670

Most Active	Vol.	Last	Chg
AmOnline	s145,937,700	57⅝	-1¼
Compaq	105,623,300	27¼	-⅛
Lucent s	80,037,500	57⁹⁄₁₆	+2⁵⁄₁₆
PhilMor	75,523,600	20⅜	-⅜
AT&T s	54,671,000	50¹¹⁄₁₆	+1⁵⁄₁₆
Citigrp s	54,304,900	54¾	-1³⁄₁₆
QwestCm	s47,619,700	43⁷⁄₈	+5⅞

Gainers	Last	Chg.	Pct.
Aeroflex	20⅜	+8¼	+68.0
ChCit pfB	ud2500	+772½	+44.7
Panavis	9¾	+2⁹⁄₁₆	+43.1
Nvolusa n	u21½	+6⅜	+42.1
LondnPac	u55	+16¼	+41.9
Gluscil L	u21³⁄₁₆	+6³⁄₁₆	+41.3
GTEF pfAcdu25⅝		+7⅜	+41.0
ICICI D n	u23⁷⁄₈	+6⁷⁄₈	+40.4

Losers	Last	Chg.	Pct.
Meditrust	d3⁷⁄₁₆	-2⁹⁄₁₆	-42.7
IntegES	d6	-2⅞	-32.4
US Food s	d12	-5¹¹⁄₁₆	-32.2
CMS Eng	d20⅜	-8¾	-30.0
AnnTayl	d16½	-5¾	-25.8
vjCrim pfF	d6⅞	-2⅜	-25.7
EnzoBio	67¾	-21½	-24.1

52 Week High	Low	Stock	Div	Yld
28½			44	

Gainers

This lists the stocks with the greatest percentage price gains for the day. It tells what the closing price was, what the actual price change was, and the percentage of change. The percentage is more important than the dollar amount of change. A $5 stock that goes up $1 has a 20% increase, while a $100 stock that goes up $1 only has a 1% increase.

Losers

This information is the opposite of the gainers. Companies hope their stocks don't make it onto this list.

UNDERSTANDING THE TICKER TAPE

*T*he ticker tape lists every trade that occurs in a stock market. Though technology has changed the form of the ticker tape from paper to electronic imagery, the information the tape provides is still the same.

TICKER TAPE TERMINOLOGY

Every stock that trades on the world's stock exchanges is identified by a short symbol (different than a stock's abbreviation you see in the newspaper stock listings). These symbols date from the days when stock trades were reported on an actual *ticker tape*. Some *ticker symbols* include a suffix to differentiate among one company's various classes of common stock.

Below is an example of what can appear on a ticker tape, although different sources, such as cable channels CNN and CNBC, may vary. When trading is very heavy and many trades must be shown as quickly as possible, the volume figure is dropped along with everything but the last dollar digit. For example, on a busy day, a trade of 25,000 CSCO at 108 will show only as "CSCO 8".

WHAT'S A "TICK?"

The term *tick* refers to a change in a stock's price from one trade to the next. It's a comparison between trades reported on the ticker. If a trade is at a higher price than the previous trade in that same stock, the trade is known as an *uptick* (because the price went up). If a trade is at a lower price than the previous trade, the trade is known as a *downtick* (because the price went down).

10sWIND58 1/4 ▲1 1/4   100sJDSU192 1/4 ▼1 1/2   40sAAPL35 ▼3/8

Up arrow
A green arrow signifies that the stock price is higher than it was when the market opened. The green number that follows tells you how much higher.

Shares traded
The first number tells you how many shares changed hands in this trade. If there is no number before the ticker symbol, it means that 100 shares were traded. The "100" means 100 round lots of 100, or 10,000 shares; the "40" means 4,000 shares.

Down arrow
A red arrow signifies that the stock price is lower than it was when the market opened. The red number that follows tells you how much lower.

ONE-LETTER TICKER SYMBOLS

Some of the largest companies listed on the NYSE have one-letter ticker symbols. Not all of the one-letter symbols are obvious, nor does the distinction mean the stock is a blue-chip company, a U.S. corporation, or even a company that's well known. Originally, when the symbol had to be written on transaction slips, it was fast to write a single letter to represent the, most heavily traded companies, such as T (Telephone), F (Ford), K (Kellogg), G (Gillette), X (US Steel), and Z (Woolworth). When Chrysler (C) was absorbed by Daimler to become DCX, Citicorp (which had just merged Citibank with Travelers) claimed the C. The Chairman of the NYSE has publicly said that he's holding the symbols "M" and "I" for two companies he hopes to convince to switch from Nasdaq to the NYSE—Microsoft and Intel.

THE OLD TICKER ▼
Before the introduction of computer technology, stock quotes were sent by wire and printed on ticker tape machines, like the one shown below. Today, the "tape" is purely a digital bar with digital numbers streaming across it.

---

24 Many websites allow you to see a ticker on your computer screen.

TICK INDICATOR

The *tick indicator* is a market indicator that helps to gauge how many stocks are moving up or down in price from their previous price and where the market may be headed. The tick indicator is computed based on the last trade in each stock.

100sCSCO10 75/8 ▲5/8   10sCSCO108 ▲3/8   90sWIND58 ▼1/4

Stock symbol
The name of a stock is referred to by its ticker symbol. Stocks on the NYSE have three letters or less. The stocks shown here trade on the Nasdaq, signified by four or more letters.

25 Unless you pay for real time service, most tickers show prices with 15 minute delays.

MEASURING PERFORMANCE

Stock market indexes (sometimes called indicators or indices) are groups of companies that are tracked and measured to interpret the movements in the stock market. Some have a narrow focus and monitor just a few companies, while others are very broad and track an entire exchange.

HOW INDEXES ARE USED

Investors mainly use indexes as tools to:

- Compare their own stock's performance with other stocks in the same category;
- Track trends in various groups of stocks and try to find buy or sell opportunities.

26 Using a broad index will give you the best look at market activity.

STOCK INDEXES

Here are some of the most common indexes used to measure the performance of various segments of the stock market. There are many more than these, allowing investors to track even small market segments.

The Dow Jones Industrial Average (DJIA). This is a group of thirty companies chosen by the editors of *The Wall Street Journal* to be reflective of the overall economy. Many investors use *The Dow* as the standard way to measure the whole market's activity, so it has become synonymous with "the stock market." Professionals don't use it as their main indicator, however, because of its narrow focus.

The Standard and Poors 500 (S&P 500). This index tracks large companies chosen by Standard and Poors (S&P), a securities rating firm. Because it tracks 500 stocks, the S&P 500 provides a more complete picture of the day's trading than The Dow.

The Russell 2000. This tracks the performance of 2,000 smaller U.S. based companies. It's designed to be a comprehensive representation of the U.S. small-cap stock market. The index consists of the smallest 2,000 companies out of the top 3,000 in domestic market capitalization.

Nasdaq Composite Index. This is the broadest index of all, measuring the performance of the entire Nasdaq, covering nearly 6,000 U.S. and foreign companies. Because many of the companies that are traded on the Nasdaq are small, young, and high tech, the Nasdaq is often seen as a barometer of investment trends.

ECONOMIC INDEXES

These indexes help identify directions in the economy.

The Index of Leading Economic Indicators. This is a collection of statistics published monthly by the Commerce Department on the level of unemployment, factory orders, and the money supply.

The Gross National Product (GNP). This is the total amount of goods and services produced by the U.S. economy each year. The GNP measures the growth of the economy. It's easiest to interpret when compared to the previous year's figures.

The Consumer Price Index (CPI). This index tracks inflation. The CPI measures the change in the prices of several hundred products such as milk, gas, cars, and homes. Prices are collected from thousands of sources making the CPI one of the broadest and most closely watched indexes.

Unemployment rates. Issued the first Friday of every month, this rate can significantly affect the movement of the market. In a strong economy, for example, an increase in employment may signal oncoming inflation and cause investors to sell some stock. In a weak economy, the same information may signal a strengthening economy and cause investors to buy more stock.

Housing starts. As the name suggests, this is the quantity of private home start-ups. It's the actual breaking of ground that begins a construction job. These figures can be one of the first signals of an upturn or downturn in the economy.

Sector indexes. These track parts (or sectors) of the economy. Many economists believe that the stock market moves in cycles and that different industry groups lead different types of market cycles, so you may learn about the strength (or weakness) of a market from who's leading and who's lagging behind.

> **27** Indexes track what has already happened. They are not a guarantee for the future.

TRACKING AN INDEX ▶
You can follow indexes like the ones shown here in your newspaper and on many websites.

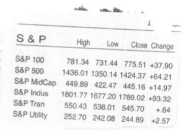

S & P	High	Low	Close	Change
S&P 100	781.34	731.44	775.51	+37.90
S&P 500	1436.01	1350.14	1424.37	+64.21
S&P MidCap	449.89	422.47	445.16	+14.97
S&P Indus	1801.77	1677.20	1789.02	+93.32
S&P Tran	550.43	538.01	545.70	+.64
S&P Utility	252.70	242.08	244.89	+2.57

PROTECTING YOURSELF

It's easy to be lured by the sound of a bargain or a "sure thing." There are, however, no guarantees in investing, and it's illegal for anyone to say otherwise. Look out for warning signs of unfair or even criminal activity.

QUESTIONABLE PRACTICES

Don't let anyone take advantage of you. Stockbrokers are legally bound by laws and regulations, which state what they can and can't do or say to get your business. Here are some things to consider.

> **28** Privately issued shares don't need approval from regulatory authorities. Proceed with caution.

DIRECT MAIL

You may receive mail offers to invest. Read these carefully. Be sure you can trust the seller, that there aren't hidden costs or questionable conditions, and that there's a phone number to reach a live person for questions.

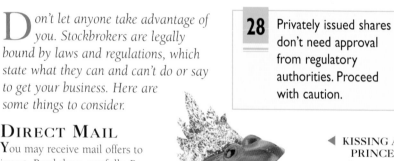

◀ **KISSING A PRINCE?**
Con artists are notoriously smooth talkers with proposals that sound almost too good to be true. In the world of investing, there are many frogs masquerading as princes (and princesses).

UNREGISTERED SECURITIES

Offering to sell securities that are not registered with the SEC can be a felony subject to a five-year federal prison term.

BUY WHAT YOU WANT

Some brokerage firms ask their brokers to push certain types of investments. This may occur if the firm is a market maker in a stock, has an investment banking relationship with the company, or wants to sell stock it owns in its own account. If you're being asked to buy stock that doesn't seem to meet your needs, you can go somewhere else. Another broker will be happy to have your business.

PHONE CALLS

Calls from unknown salespeople, called *cold calls*, are common these days. Be wary. How did they get your name? What company do they work for? Never provide personal or financial information over the phone. Either hang up or ask to receive literature by mail. Reputable salespeople will be able to give you as much information as you need to verify their legitimacy and won't be evasive. It may be best to believe the call is a scam until clearly proven otherwise.

DON'T RUSH

If someone says you've got to buy now before the price jumps up, be careful. Short-term speculation is a dangerous game for beginning investors. Many have taken advice and been burned. Ask for research to help you decide, and remember: Stocks that rise dramatically in a short period are usually speculative stocks with high risk levels.

FREQUENT TRADING

Churning is an illegal practice where a broker leads clients to buy and sell frequently in order to increase commissions. If you feel your broker is doing this, report it to the branch manager of your brokerage firm. If you don't get a satisfactory response, take your claim higher (see pgs. 68-69) and find another broker.

29 Don't invest in anything you don't understand. Ask for information.

KNOW YOUR RIGHTS

As a shareholder, you have certain rights and privileges. You're entitled to receive information from the company on its activities at specific times and you may be asked to vote on issues facing the company.

SHAREHOLDERS HAVE RIGHTS

Shareholders have specific rights by law and under the company's bylaws.

Information. Shares that are *publicly listed* on stock exchanges are required to provide information or *disclosure* to their shareholders in return for being publicly traded. This means that as a shareholder, you are entitled to receive reports quarterly (every 3 months) and annually (once a year) to keep you informed of the company's performance and status.

In case of bankruptcy. If the company goes bankrupt, you have the right to share in any money that remains after all other creditors who have superior claims to your's have been repaid.

Shareholder rights plans. These plans are created by company management to protect the business from hostile takeovers. Typically, they create a way for current shareholders to purchase more shares at lower prices.

SHAREHOLDERS HAVE PRIVILEGES

The shareholders vote to elect the directors of a company who appoint the company's management and set the dividend policy. Shareholders may also attend company meetings and vote on specific company policies presented there. For every share of stock you own, you have one vote—as long as the type of stock you own has voting rights.

PRIORITIZING YOUR RIGHTS

It's important to know the different types of investments you can make in a company and how that company prioritizes each one. This will help you know which investors will be paid, and in what order, in case the company goes bankrupt.

Loans are debt. They're repaid completely before any other distributions;

Bonds are debt. Bondholders are repaid before stockholders;

Preferred stock is shareholders equity. Preferred stockholders are only paid after bondholders are fully repaid;

Common stock is shareholders equity. Common stockholders are paid only after everyone else is paid in full.

HOW DO YOU VOTE?

Whenever there's an issue that needs to be voted on, the company whose stock you own will send you a *proxy* (a sample is shown below). A proxy is simply a ballot. You're asked to check off whether you're for, against, or abstaining from voting on the issue. Then you mail the proxy back to the company in the envelope they give you.

PROXY ▶

Your brokerage firm may receive your proxy and pass it on to you. If a company has a record of you as a shareholder and has your name and address, it may send the proxy directly to you.

30 The more shares you own, the more power and influence you have on the decisions affecting the company.

INTERNET VOTING

At many companies, you can vote your shares via the Internet. The instructions for web-based voting are usually provided with your proxy. It's very easy, quick, and doesn't require a trip to the post office.

CAUTION – MAKE SURE YOU'RE INSURED

Any brokerage firm, its clearing agents, and the holding companies that hold your assets in *street-name* should be insured with the Security Investor's Protection Corporation (SIPC). This is a government agency that safeguards against the failure of your brokerage firm. If the firm has SIPC insurance and it goes bankrupt, your money is insured. You may pay an SEC "tax" on any trade you make. A firm may add this fee to your trade to defray miscellaneous expenses. If a broker goes bankrupt it's the only thing that prevents a total loss. Investigate thoroughly!

PROTECT YOUR RIGHTS

If you have a problem with your broker or a trade, you do have rights. There are government organizations and laws that regulate all organizations and activities associated with trading stocks. These agencies are in place to protect investors from fraudulent and illegal activities. Here is what you can do and who you can call to protect your rights.

WHAT YOU CAN DO

Act quickly. The time to resolve problems is often limited by law. Check with the SEC if you need to know the specific amount of time you have to resolve an issue.

Call first. First talk to your broker and explain the problem. Taking notes of conversations can help resolve issues more quickly. If your broker can't resolve the problem, ask to speak to the branch manager.

Then write. If the problem remains unresolved, write to the compliance department at the firm's home office. Explain your problem clearly and tell how you want it resolved. Ask the compliance office to respond to you in writing within 30 days. If you're still not satisfied, send a letter to, or call one of the agencies that oversees your brokerage firm, such as the SEC or NASD. Include copies of any important documents or letters you've already written.

The agency will research your complaint, contact the firm or person you've complained about and ask them to respond to your issues. Sometimes, just their initial contact resolves the problem.

If these steps don't work, you may need to take legal action on your own. The SEC and NASD can send you information on mediation or arbitration and suggest how to locate a lawyer if you need one.

Preventive measures. Federal or state securities laws require brokers, and their firms to be licensed or registered, and to make important information public. But it's up to you to find that information and use it to protect your investment dollars. The good news is that this information is easy to get, and one phone call may save you from sending your money to a con artist, a bad broker, or disreputable firm. Before you invest, see that your broker is licensed to sell securities and whether they or their firms have had run-ins with regulators or other investors. Call 800-289-9999, toll-free.

WHO TO CALL

The Securities and Exchange Commission (SEC).

The SEC regulates information disclosure to investors so that everyone has equal access to information and is protected through the proper functioning of the stock markets. It also regulates all exchange members, brokers, investment advisors, stock exchanges, mutual funds, and public utility holding companies, and prohibits manipulative trading practices such as insider trading.

The National Association of Securities Dealers (NASD).

The NASD regulates the behavior of its member securities dealers. It develops rules and regulations, conducts regulatory reviews of members' business activities, disciplines violators, and designs and regulates securities markets and services. In addition, it owns and operates Nasdaq. The NASD gets its authority from the SEC, and requires that every securities dealer in the country be a member of its organization.

State regulators. Most states have their own regulatory agencies. Each state requires all securities sold within its borders to be registered. They also require all stockbrokers and brokerage firms conducting business within their state to be licensed.

Private organizations. The SEC has designated various private organizations to operate and oversee aspects of the securities business. These organizations are called *self-regulatory organizations*.

Self-regulatory Organizations (SROs).

The largest SRO is the NASD. All these agencies work to provide investors with accurate, reliable information about securities, maintain ethical standards, and prevent fraud against investors.

Professional regulators. As part of its registration process, NASD Regulation reviews each applicant's employment and disciplinary histories for any evidence that might disqualify him or her from selling securities to the public. Applicants must also have their fingerprints submitted to the FBI for a criminal record check and pass a series of comprehensive examinations.

PUBLIC RECORDS

The *Central Registration Depository* (CRD) is a computerized database that contains information about most brokers, some investment advisors, their representatives, and the firms they work for. For instance, you can find out if brokers are properly licensed in your state and if they have had run-ins with regulators or received serious complaints from investors. You will also find information about the brokers' educational backgrounds and where they've worked before their current jobs. You can ask your state securities regulator or the National Association of Securities Dealers (NASD) to provide you with information from the CRD.

INDEX

ACKNOWLEDGMENTS

AUTHORS' ACKNOWLEDGMENTS

The production of this book has called on the skills of many people. A special thanks to
Robert A. "Rocky" Mills, Senior Vice President at Sutro & Co. in Woodland Hills, California.
Rocky's considerable expertise in investments, garnered from over 20 years as a wealth management
advisor, branch director, and Wall Street executive, played an important role in keeping this book
current and in line with "real world" thinking. We would like particularly to mention our
editors at Dorling Kindersley, and our consultant, Nick Clemente. Marc wishes to dedicate
this book to Zachary Robinson for his great patience and support when it was most needed.

PUBLISHER'S ACKNOWLEDGMENTS

Dorling Kindersley would like to thank everyone who worked on the
Essential Finance series, and the following for their help and participation:

Editorial Stephanie Rubenstein; **Design and Layout** Hedayat Sandjari;
Consultants Nick Clemente; Skeeter; **Indexer** Rachel Rice; **Proofreader** Stephanie Rubenstein;
Photography Anthony Nex; **Photographers' Assistants** Stephanie Fowler;
Models Kristine Nex, Richard Tohl, Federico Barbier, Kay Livesley, Eleanor Rose, Harold Rose,
Kara Rubenstein, Zachary Robinson, Jennifer Issa; **Picture Researcher** Mark Dennis; Sam Ruston

Special thanks to Teresa Clavasquin for her generous support and assistance.

AUTHOR'S BIOGRAPHY

Marc Robinson is co-founder of Internet-based moneytours.com, a personal finance resource for
corporations, universities, credit unions, and other institutions interested in helping their
constituents make intelligent decisions about their financial lives. He wrote the original
The Wall Street Journal Guide to Understanding Money and Markets, created *The Wall Street Journal
Guide to Understanding Personal Finance*, co-published a personal finance series with
Time Life Books, and wrote a children's book about onomateopia in different languages. In his
two decades in the financial services industry, Marc has provided marketing consulting
to many top Wall Street firms. He is admitted to practice law in New York State.